Meet the Authors

Dr Felicity Baker and Dr Jo Burrell

Welcome to our Little Book of HR Resilience.

As clinical psychologists and researchers working with businesses, we've spent over a decade transforming workplace wellbeing through evidence-based psychological solutions.

We are now on a mission to ensure HR professionals also receive the recognition, support, and strategies they need to stay mentally healthy and thrive in their roles.

We believe that a resilient HR function is the foundation of resilient workplaces — and its wellbeing matters now more than ever.

Jo & Felicity

Why Resilience Matters for HR Professionals

HR professionals are the emotional anchor of an organisation, supporting others whilst navigating complexity and competing demands. Yet their own wellbeing is often overlooked.

Our 2025 HR Mental Wellbeing Survey* revealed the impact of this on HR practitioners and on the profession as a whole:

- 63% of HR practitioners are suffering burnout.
- 42% are actively considering leaving the profession.

We believe it's time for change. The mental wellbeing crisis in HR needs urgent solutions:

- Organisations must commit to providing regular support, tailored to the unique needs of HR.
- HR professionals need help to grow personal resilience.

Together, these two measures will equip HR to bounce back from challenges and perform at their best.

*Get in touch to read the full report:
Enquiries@ultimateresilience.co.uk

This Little Book of HR Resilience is just one step in our campaign to improve the working lives of HR professionals.

Here, we share evidence-based techniques to help you build resilience, protect your mental health, and prevent burnout.

We're committed to safeguarding your wellbeing, so you can keep making a difference in the profession you love.

> *The greatest glory in living lies not in never falling, but in rising every time we fall.*
> **Nelson Mandela**

How to use this book

There's a lot of content!

Take your time.
Pick one or two strategies to try.
Discover what works for you.

Our Top Strategies to Boost Resilience

1. Know yourself, tame stress
- Spot stress early　　　　　　　　　　　　8
- Soothe threat emotions　　　　　　　　11
- Prioritise breaks to boost productivity　13

2. Build emotional strengths
- Spot & savour positive emotions　　　　16
- Bring back your sparkle　　　　　　　　18

3. Foster meaningful connections
- Grow your circle of support   20
- Seek expert guidance   22
- Harness self-compassion   23
- Connect with kindness   24
- Cultivate quality conversations   25
- Firm up your boundaries   26

4. Face challenges with confidence
- Banish self-imposed pressure   30
- Conquer your inner imposter   31
- Block burnout   32
- Build skills to thrive   34

1

KNOW YOURSELF, TAME STRESS

Spot stress early

Feelings of stress and overwhelm make it hard for you to function as normal.

Commonly known as the fight-or-flight response, stress symptoms can manifest as:

- **Emotional**: Heightened anger, irritability, or anxiety, overwhelming urges to escape or avoid certain situations.
- **Cognitive**: Reduced focus and concentration.
- **Physical:** Muscle tension, over-breathing, increased heart rate, or a churning stomach.

Recognising these signs as soon as they emerge is the first and most important step you can take to stop stress in its tracks.

WHAT ARE YOUR EARLY WARNING SIGNS OF STRESS?

THINK OF THE LAST TIME YOU FELT OVERWHELMED OR STRESSED

WHAT WAS THE SITUATION?

WHAT BODY SENSATIONS DID YOU NOTICE?

WHAT EMOTIONS DID YOU FEEL?

WHAT DID YOU THINK?

WHAT DID YOU DO?

These are your early warning signs of stress. What are some common scenarios that can trigger these symptoms?

Choose how to respond

Knowing your triggers and recognising your typical early warning signs of stress opens up choices about how to manage and respond.

Think of it like a traffic light:
- **Red**: Stop - when you notice stress
- **Amber**: Reflect - on how to respond
- **Green:** Take action

It might feel like you don't have a choice when you are under pressure. But there are many strategies that will help.

Our tips and techniques will help you soothe stress emotions in the moment and boost positive emotions going forwards.

For example, learning to manage negative thinking and self-imposed pressure will support you to *change how you feel by changing how you think*.

Prioritising self-care, connecting with loved-ones and hobbies will allow you to *reconnect with what you love in life* and boost resilience.

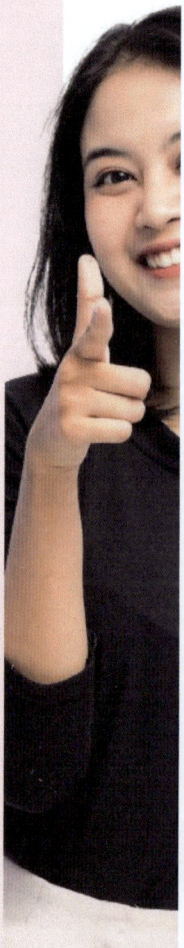

Soothe threat emotions

Calming threat emotions can quickly reduce stress.

Using a simple slow rhythmic breathing technique is a **TOP stress buster!**

In just a few moments, it will soothe the fight-or-flight response, calm your body, and free your mind to start problem-solving.

And it is so unobtrusive that you can use it anywhere: in meetings, in the car, even when you are doing a presentation.

> *Based on powerful physiological research, this technique works by rebalancing the oxygen and carbon dioxide in your body and regulating your heart rate.*

TRY THE SLOW RHYTHMIC BREATHING TECHNIQUE

Find a space where you feel relaxed and won't be disturbed.

1. Breathe in slowly over a count of 4 seconds.
2. Breathe out for a longer count of 6 seconds.
3. Pause briefly at the end of the out-breath.
4. Repeat.

Practising for 5 minutes per day for two weeks will help you master this technique.

> *If you struggle with this or find you are are running out of breath try:*
> - *Changing the ratio of in to out breaths to suit you (e.g. 3 seconds in, 5 seconds out).*
> - *Imagine you are breathing out through a straw.*

Prioritise breaks to boost productivity

When you feel overwhelmed, skipping breaks might feel productive, but it often backfires.

Without rest, decision-making falters, productivity dips, and stress mounts.

Recharge and Refocus

- Schedule downtime for relaxation, hobbies, or connecting with friends.
- Spend time away from screens.
- Engage in nourishing activities - like watching a movie, taking a walk, or pursuing a creative hobby.

Taking time out during the day - even short breaks - will soothe stress and boost focus and productivity.

> *Tip: Make your work diary work for you! Try shortening meetings and calls to create space for a breather, to reflect, re-group, or prepare.*

GIVE YOUR BRAIN A BREAK

WHEN YOU NOTICE YOUR EARLY WARNING SIGNS OF STRESS, STEP BACK AND TRY THIS RESET EXERCISE TO IDENTIFY WHAT IS DEPLETING YOU AND WHAT WILL NOURISH YOU:

WRITE DOWN WHAT IS DRAINING YOU RIGHT NOW?

WHAT DO YOU NEED TO BE DOING? WHAT'S URGENT RIGHT NOW?

WHAT DO YOU NEED RIGHT NOW? WHAT WILL NOURISH YOU?

Remember, taking breaks is an investment in your resilience and wellbeing.

2

BUILD EMOTIONAL STRENGTHS

> *Positive emotions broaden our awareness and build our resourcefulness, paving the way for resilience and wellbeing.*
> **Barbara Fredrickson**

Spot & savour positive emotions

Emotions like amusement, joy and interest stimulate the parasympathetic nervous system, creating a sense of calm and soothing the stress response.

We have evolved to pay more attention to negative emotions because these protect us from threat. Positive emotions can be harder to notice as they don't grab our attention in the same way.

So we have to work harder to be aware of them.

Try jotting down **three good things** that happen each day - like sharing a laugh with friends, enjoying a tasty meal, or witnessing a beautiful sunset.

 Reflecting on these moments, especially before bed, can ease stress and improve sleep quality.

THREE GOOD THINGS JOURNAL

3 GOOD THINGS THAT HAPPENED TODAY

SOMETHING I'M PROUD OF

TOMORROW I LOOK FORWARD TO

Bring back your sparkle

When you are under pressure, struggling with demands and feeling overwhelmed you can easily let the things you enjoy take a back seat.

Actively seeking out 'sparkling moments' in your day will help you to open your mind to positive emotions and to harness all the benefits they bring.

Try our **28 Day Sparkling Moments Challenge**.

Engaging in these exercises regularly will generate more sparkling moments in your life, boosting your resilience and wellbeing!

Record them in your **Sparkling Moments Diary** (Appendix p.37) to keep positive emotions in focus and as a reminder when you are having a difficult day.

3

FOSTER MEANINGFUL CONNECTIONS

Grow your circle of support

Strong, supportive relationships are crucial for resilience and wellbeing. But stress and overwhelm can lead to social withdrawal, making it harder to access support.

Talking with someone impartial and non-judgmental can calm stress symptoms, allowing you to think clearly and problem-solve effectively.

Grow Your Tribe
- Aim for face to face contact where possible.
- Celebrate successes.
- Find ways to appreciate and value each other.
- Share concerns with trusted friends or colleagues.
- Seek professional support through **HR supervision** or mentoring.

REVIEW YOUR SOCIAL NETWORK

WRITE THE NAMES OF PEOPLE IN YOUR SOCIAL NETWORK AT HOME AND WORK AND THOSE THAT CROSS OVER.

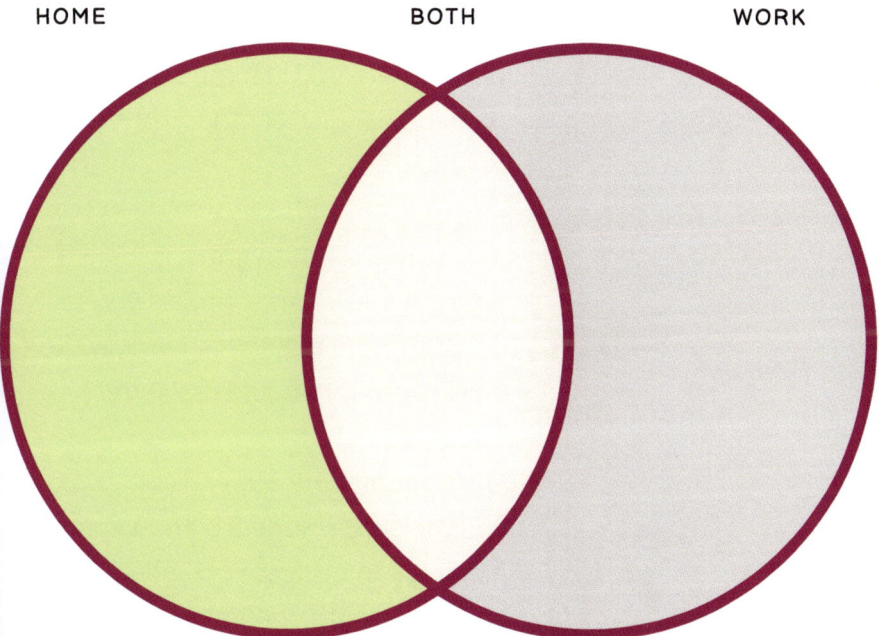

Ask yourself:
- How do I gain support, and from whom?
- How do I offer support and to whom?
- Is there a good balance of giving and receiving?
- Is there space for you both to express your thoughts and feelings?
- Do they accept and value things about you, and you them?
- Can they see things from your perspective without judgement and vice versa?
- Which relationships are less well-balanced or problematic?

Seek expert guidance

You're holding everyone else together. *HR Supervision holds you together*

Find out more about HR supervision

Supervision is a dedicated, impartial place where you can reflect, recharge, and strengthen your practice.

It empowers you to grow professionally and supports you to be happy and healthy at work, while staying grounded and resilient.

Our specialist HR Supervision gives you the space, support, and expert guidance to navigate complex challenges with confidence.

So you can protect your own mental health while helping others to thrive.

> *When we prioritise our wellbeing, everything else in our life gets better, including our products, including our performance at work, including our success.*
> **Arianna Huffington**

Harness self-compassion

At times of stress, it can be easy to slip into self-criticism.

Thoughts like "I'm not good enough," "I'm rubbish at my job," or "People think I'm incompetent" create a vicious cycle that fuels further stress.

Being kind to yourself provides an exit strategy.

Break the Cycle
Counteract negative thoughts by remembering times when you achieved targets. overcame challenges or received positive feedback.

Spend Time with Loved-ones
People who value and care about you will help to remind you of your strengths.

Practice Mindfulness
Stimulate acceptance of yourself and grow self-compassion through the practice of mindfulness.

 No act of kindness, no matter how small, is ever wasted.
Aesop

Connect with kindness

Being shown kindness triggers endorphins and oxytocin that help to soothe us and contribute to feelings of contentment and safety. But the benefits of kindness are not limited to those receiving it.

The *performance* of kind acts has been associated with enhanced life satisfaction in the giver as well as the receiver.

 A little kindness goes a long way

Surprise someone with a random act of kindness!

However small - holding the door open, washing someone's dishes or offering to walk their dog - research shows doing this will improve your mood and enhance feelings of connection.

Cultivate quality conversations

Connecting with friends and colleagues is known to have a hugely positive impact on wellbeing.

And yet, opportunities for social interaction have taken a hit with the rise of remote and hybrid working.

Making time for just one quality conversation each day can significantly boost your wellbeing.

It doesn't matter what you talk about either:
- Catching up
- A deep and meaningful exchange
- Joking around
- Offering support or care
- Listening
- Showing appreciation or valuing someone else's opinion

A quality conversation will help you manage stress, focus on what matters in your life and keep work in perspective.

> *Just the act of intentionally reaching out to a colleague or loved-one each day could make all the difference.*

Firm up your boundaries

Are the words 'Can you just...' familiar to you?

How often are you asked to do something you don't have time for, is outside your job description, or you don't have training for?

The expectation that you are always available and will pick up anything that's thrown at you can push you outside your comfort zone and increase stress.

Set your boundaries . . .

- Communicate response times, clearly define your working hours and availability.
- **Work within your expertise** - be direct with others if their requests are outside your remit.
- **Use assertiveness** say no to non-essential tasks or to prioritise urgent matters.
- Be wary of blurring the boundary between personal and professional relationships.
- Build skills to **navigate sensitive conversations** confidently at work.

BEING ASSERTIVE

What are your barriers to being assertive?

UNHELPFUL BELIEFS ABOUT ASSERTIVENESS

- [ ] I shouldn't challenge authority
- [ ] I will upset the other person
- [ ] They wont like me if I say no
- [ ] I don't want to make a fuss
- [ ] My needs don't matter
- [ ] I don't want to get into conflict
- [ ] It'll be easier if I do it myself
- [ ] They'll think I'm overreacting

WHAT'S A MORE HELPFUL WAY OF THINKING?

TRY

The 'rain check no'

Saying 'Let me think about it', or 'I'll have to check my diary and get back to you' in responses to requests.

This buys you time to consider, is this something you:
a) Want to do
b) Have the skills to do
c) Have time & resources to do

The 'broken record technique'

- Repeat your message like a broken record.
- Stick to your point.
- Don't get drawn into negotiations aimed at wearing you down.

Useful where you fear criticism or may be distracted by clever but irrelevant arguments.

7 STEPS TO NAVIGATE SENSITIVE CONVERSATIONS CONFIDENTLY

1. Don't avoid the conversation - *Ignoring issues can make things worse or create difficulties for you further down the line.*

2. Create the right environment - *Choose a private, quiet, and neutral space for the conversation. This helps reduce anxiety, minimise distractions, and ensures focus is on the topic at hand.*

3. Set boundaries - *Clarify your role and purpose of the meeting. Establish confidentiality and its limits to build trust and safety.*

4. Listen actively & without judgment - *Use open body language, avoid interrupting, and reflect back what you hear. Listening well helps the person feel seen, heard, and valued.*

5. Focus on impact, not fixing - *You're not there to solve personal problems — Stay focused on the work context and explore the support they need to deal with it..*

6. Collaborate on next steps - *Work together to identify practical, tailored solutions. Agree on a plan, including a follow-up review to establish any further steps needed.*

7. Signpost to available resources - *Share information about helpful sources of information or support.*

4

FACE CHALLENGES WITH CONFIDENCE

Banish self-imposed pressure

Unrealistic expectations and perfectionism can quickly spiral into self-criticism, stress, and anxiety.

Recognising and reframing these patterns is key.

Try using **flexible thinking techniques**:
1. Notice when your thoughts become harsh or negative.
2. Weigh up the evidence: Are these thoughts based on fact or are they overly self-critical?
3. Identify balanced, realistic perspectives.

Try evaluating your negative thoughts with the support of a friend or colleague. This will help to calm the stress you feel, allowing you to more easily find new perspectives.

> *Finding balanced ways of thinking in challenging situations helps you banish self-imposed pressure to stay emotionally and physically calm.*

Conquer your inner imposter

If you're struggling with a **persistent fear of being "found out"**, not being good enough or a belief that someone else could do your job better, you're not alone.

This pattern of negative thinking is associated with **Imposter Syndrome**. It feeds self-doubt, undermines your confidence and contributes to burnout.

Try noticing when you are thinking this way and:
- **Fight back** against your inner critic. Use your Three Good Things Journal to remember times you were proud of yourself or received positive feedback.
- Use **flexible thinking skills** to develop a more balanced view of yourself.
- **Let go of perfectionism** and allow yourself to set realistic goals.
- **Become your inner cheerleader,** celebrate successes and believe in yourself.

> *Adopting a growth mindset is all about embracing challenges - viewing setbacks as opportunities for learning, rather than confirmation of your perceived flaws.*

Block burnout

Chronic stress, persistent challenge and high pressure can all contribute to burnout.

Striving - working harder and longer, but being less productive.
Questioning - doubting your skills and ability to cope.
Languishing - becoming increasingly negative, denying that you are struggling, despite others expressing concern about you.
Losing Control - normal coping mechanisms stop working, rising overwhelm, anxiety and low mood.
Crisis - complete emotional, physical, and mental exhaustion, feelings of dread, a loss of interest and motivation.

Building self-awareness of your early warning signs of burnout and taking action to manage stress early , will help to prevent the slippery slide into burnout.

ARE YOU AT RISK OF BURNOUT?

COMPLETE THIS QUESTIONNAIRE* TO FIND OUT

INDICATE HOW OFTEN EACH STATEMENT APPLIES TO YOU.

	NEVER 1	RARELY 2	SOMETIMES 3	OFTEN 4	ALWAYS 5
AT WORK I FEEL MENTALLY EXHAUSTED	☐	☐	☐	☐	☐
I STRUGGLE TO FIND ANY ENTHUSIASM FOR MY WORK	☐	☐	☐	☐	☐
WHEN I'M WORKING, I HAVE TROUBLE CONCENTRATING	☐	☐	☐	☐	☐
AT WORK I MAY OVERREACT UNINTENTIONALLY	☐	☐	☐	☐	☐

Add together all your scores and then divide by the number of items completed to find out your total.

What your total score means:
2.53 or less = No risk of burnout
2.54 to 2.95 = At risk of burnout
2.96 or more = Burnout very likely

> *If you are at risk of burnout, taking action now can pull you back from the brink. Try confiding in a loved one or trusted colleague or seek professional guidance. Reaching out will help you address external pressures and hone your coping skills.*

*Schaufeli, W.B., De Witte, H. & Desart, S. (2020). Manual Burnout Assessment Tool (BAT) – Version 2.0. KU Leuven, Belgium: Unpublished internal report

Build skills to thrive

Stress and burnout don't just undermine your wellbeing, they also erode your capacity to foster a healthy workplace culture. That's why it's not enough to simply manage stress.

By actively broadening your resilience toolkit - from emotion regulation and cognitive flexibility, to self-care and connection - you'll become better equipped not just to survive, but to thrive.

And by building your resiilience toolkit you'll be able to:
- **Lead by example**, showing your team the value of self-care and psychological safety.
- **Stay grounded** and make sound decisions under pressure.
- **Drive initiatives** that promote organisational resilience and sustainable wellbeing.

TAKE YOUR RESILIENCE TO THE NEXT LEVEL

Your role is vital and so is your health.

Developing a full set of resilience skills isn't just about surviving the demands of your role.

It's about thriving, personally and professionally, while supporting others to do the same.

The Essential Resilience E-learning programme:
All the evidence-based strategies you need for sustainable resilience.

Use the QR code to start boosting your resilience

Enter: HR-LITTLEBOOK at checkout to claim your 50% discount

Dr Felicity Baker & Dr Jo Burrell

Join our campaign to #MakeHRHappyAgain

APPENDIX

SPARKLING MOMENTS CHALLENGE

Discover and savour your 'sparkling moments' by actively seeking out experiences that revive your enjoyment and enthusiasm

28 DAY SPARKLING MOMENTS CHALLENGE

DAY 1 WRITE DOWN THREE THINGS YOU ARE GRATEFUL FOR TODAY.

DAY 2 TAKE A MOMENT TO APPRECIATE SOMETHING IN NATURE - A BEAUTIFUL VIEW OR THE FEELING OF THE SUN ON YOUR SKIN.

28 DAY SPARKLING MOMENTS CHALLENGE

DAY 3 WRITE ABOUT A MOMENT OR EXPERIENCE THAT MADE YOU FEEL GRATEFUL OR BLESSED.

DAY 4 WRITE ABOUT A LOVED ONE WHO HAS SUPPORTED YOU AND HOW THEY HAVE POSITIVELY IMPACTED YOUR LIFE.

28 DAY SPARKLING MOMENTS CHALLENGE

DAY 5 WRITE ABOUT A TIME SOMEONE SHOWED YOU KINDNESS AND HOW IT AFFECTED YOUR LIFE.

DAY 6 WRITE ABOUT A CHALLENGE OR OBSTACLE THAT TAUGHT YOU SOMETHING IMPORTANT.

28 DAY SPARKLING MOMENTS CHALLENGE

DAY 7 WRITE ABOUT A TEACHER OR MENTOR WHO HAS POSITIVELY IMPACTED OR INFLUENCED YOUR LIFE.

DAY 8 CALL OR TEXT SOMEONE TO LET THEM KNOW WHY YOU APPRECIATE THEM.

28 DAY SPARKLING MOMENTS CHALLENGE

DAY 9 WRITE ABOUT A PLACE YOU ARE GRATEFUL FOR - E.G. YOUR HOME, A FAVORITE VACATION SPOT, OR A COSY COFFEE SHOP.

DAY 10 TAKE A MOMENT TO WRITE ABOUT THREE THINGS YOU ARE THANKFUL FOR REGARDING YOUR HEALTH.

28 DAY SPARKLING MOMENTS CHALLENGE

DAY 11 MAKE A LIST OF FIVE THINGS YOU ARE LOOKING FORWARD TO IN THE FUTURE.

DAY 12 WRITE ABOUT A SPIRITUAL BELIEF OR PRACTICE THAT BRINGS YOU PEACE.

28 DAY SPARKLING MOMENTS CHALLENGE

DAY 13 MAKE A LIST OF TEN THINGS YOU ARE GRATEFUL FOR IN YOUR WORK.

DAY 14 WRITE ABOUT THREE THINGS THAT MAKE YOU LAUGH OR SMILE.

28 DAY SPARKLING MOMENTS CHALLENGE

DAY 15 WRITE ABOUT A PERSON WHO HAS POSITIVELY IMPACTED YOUR LIFE AT WORK.

DAY 16 WRITE ABOUT A TALENT OR SKILL YOU HAVE THAT YOU ARE GRATEFUL FOR AND HOW IT BENEFITS YOU.

28 DAY SPARKLING MOMENTS CHALLENGE

DAY 17 WRITE ABOUT A PERSONAL POSSESSION THAT BRINGS YOU JOY.

DAY 18 TAKE A MOMENT TO WRITE ABOUT SOMETHING YOU ARE THANKFUL FOR IN YOUR COMMUNITY.

28 DAY SPARKLING MOMENTS CHALLENGE

DAY 19 TAKE A MOMENT TO RECOGNISE THE TECHNOLOGY YOU USE AND WRITE ABOUT HOW IT POSITIVELY IMPACTS YOUR LIFE.

DAY 20 WRITE ABOUT A PET OR ANIMAL THAT BRINGS JOY TO YOUR LIFE.

28 DAY SPARKLING MOMENTS CHALLENGE

DAY 21 WRITE ABOUT A HISTORICAL FIGURE OR EVENT THAT HAS POSITIVELY IMPACTED YOUR LIFE.

DAY 22 MAKE A LIST OF FIVE THINGS THAT BRING YOU JOY.

28 DAY SPARKLING MOMENTS CHALLENGE

DAY 23 WRITE A THANK-YOU NOTE TO SOMEONE WHO HAS MADE A DIFFERENCE IN YOUR LIFE.

DAY 24 TAKE A MOMENT TO APPRECIATE YOUR JOB OR CAREER AND WRITE ABOUT HOW IT HAS POSITIVELY IMPACTED YOUR LIFE.

28 DAY SPARKLING MOMENTS CHALLENGE

DAY 25 WRITE ABOUT A BOOK OR MOVIE THAT HAS INSPIRED YOU.

DAY 26 WRITE ABOUT A DELICIOUS FOOD OR MEAL AND WHY IT BRINGS YOU JOY.

28 DAY SPARKLING MOMENTS CHALLENGE

DAY 27 TAKE A MOMENT TO APPRECIATE YOUR FAVOURITE SMELL AND WRITE ABOUT YOUR EXPERIENCE.

DAY 28 MAKE A LIST OF THREE THINGS YOU ARE GRATEFUL FOR REGARDING TO YOUR PERSONAL GROWTH OR DEVELOPMENT.

Printed in Great Britain
by Amazon